To Be a Student
Vocation and Leisure in Service to Neighbor

By Scott A. Ashmon
and Scott L. Keith

To Be a Student
© 2016 New Reformation Publications

Published by:
New Reformation Publications
PO Box 54032
Irvine, CA 92619-4032

Printed in the United States of America

ISBN: 978-1-945500-86-2 Soft Cover
ISBN: 978-1-945500-87-9 E-book

NRP Books is committed to packaging and promoting the finest
content for fueling a new Lutheran Reformation. We promote the
defense of the Christian faith, confessional Lutheran theology,
vocation and civil courage.

The Vocation of Student

What does it mean to be a student? Several responses can be given to this simple, yet complex, question. The place to begin with is the observation that to be a student—like to be a daughter or a son, a brother or a sister, a friend or a citizen—is to have a vocation. This is apparent in the fact that this university has accepted your application for enrollment. In doing so, the university has called you, placing upon you the honorable and holy vocation of student.

It might sound strange to say that being a student is honorable and holy, but it is. It is much more than, as many people think, a path to a profession or financial well-being. While vocations come to us through human agents and physical means, they originally and ultimately are placed upon us by God through creation and redemption. The book of Genesis records in chapters 1 and 2 that when God created mankind—male and female—in His image, He gave them certain functions to perform: namely, to have dominion over the earth as God's royal stewards and to procreate as husband and wife in order to bring forth more children of God, bearing His image, on the earth to care for it and each other.

Implicit in this vocation is that what all people do, think, or say should be very good, just as God created the rest of the cosmos to be "very good," because, by His nature, He is "very good." In other words, humans were made in God's image to do good, both for the natural world and each other. They were created and called to love as God first loved them. All people have this creation-based calling from God, even though, as Genesis 3 recounts, humanity fell into open rebellion against God and broke their God-given image, bringing the vices of selfishness, harm, injustice, and wickedness into God's world.

Still, God continued to call people to bless and serve His beloved creatures. For instance, God calls Abram in Genesis 12 to be the father of many nations and promises Abram that, through him, God would bless all nations. Later, in Leviticus 25, God calls Israel to care for the Promised Land He has graciously gifted to them, just as that land cares for them; God calls Israel to give the land rest every seventh year, as God has given them rest in Him. Centuries later, in Isaiah 45, we see God preordaining King Cyrus of Persia, a polytheist who did not worship God, to be God's "messiah" to deliver His people to Judah out of foreign captivity so that they could return to the Promised Land.

This Is God's Call

God's call continues in the New Testament with deliverance from sin and death won by God's Son, Jesus Christ. As Gene Veith rightly observes, "Scripture is full of passages that describe how we have been *called* to faith through the Gospel (e.g., 2 Thessalonians 2:14)" and "how God *calls* us to a particular office or way of life (e.g., 1 Corinthians 1:1–2, 7:15–20)."[1] God calls each person to salvation through faith in Christ (1 Timothy 2:3–7). Those who do not reject this calling, but receive this gracious gift of faith and redemption, are then called to love and do good to their neighbors as Christ first loved them (Ephesian 2:8–10; 1 John 4:9–11). This loving-kindness toward neighbors near and far is not the precondition for salvation but the fruits of it.

So what does this have to do with being a student? To be a student is to have a vocation, and all true vocations are holy and honorable callings placed upon people by God in creation and redemption. Each vocation is not only a God-given role but a way for people to respond in kind to God's good and gracious gifts by being merciful and beneficial to their neighbors—both people and nature. As Veith succinctly summarizes it, "*The purpose of vocation is to love and serve one's neighbor.*"[2] If being a student is a vocation, then all that you think, say, and do as a student should be seen through this lens. This is precisely what theologian Stanley Hauerwas of Duke University lays out in an open letter to college students: "To be a student is to be called to serve the Church and the world. . . . You are called to the life

---

1. Gene Edward Veith, Jr., *God at Work: Your Christian Vocation in All of Life* (Wheaton, IL: Crossway, 2002), 17.

2. Veith, *God at Work*, 39–40.

of the mind to be of service."[3] The purpose of being a student is to love and serve one's neighbor for their temporal and eternal well-being.

Vocation as Love of Neighbor

How should you love your neighbor as a student? You might immediately jump to the idea of service projects or mission trips. True, these are ways to love others while being a student. But you can do those quite apart from being a student. So the question still remains: How can you love others through your calling as a student??

It might be a shock to the system to say this, but the first way to love others as a student is . . . to study. Leland Ryken, president emeritus of Wheaton College, emphasizes this point to students when he says, "Learning, in whatever form, *is* the student's calling."[4] This statement would seem self-evident since the noun "student" comes from the Latin verb *studeō*, which means "to be devoted to, lay stress on, study." This might seem not only obvious etymologically but a bit bland. Love, after all, is a verb, a transitive, active verb.

---

3. Stanley Hauerwas, "Go with God: An Open Letter to Young Christians on Their Way to College," *First Things* 207 (November 2010): 50–51.

4. Leland Ryken, "The Student's Calling," in *Liberal Arts for the Christian Life*, eds. Jeffry C. Davis and Philip G. Ryken (Wheaton, IL: Crossway, 2012), 21,

Studying is not much of an activity that impacts others, or so it seems.

One might say that studying, learning all that one can and gaining all the wisdom possible, *will* one day result in a loving activity. For instance, studying will lead to a degree, which will lead to a job, which will lead to money, which will allow you to care for your family and give to others. This is true, but all vocations have a "here and now" vitality to them, not just a "there and then" eventuality.[5] This means that the calling of student must also have a present activity of love and service for others.

Three Ps

This present activity is expressed well in a chapter penned by Korey Maas. Maas talks about the three Ps students serve in studying: parents, peers, and professors.[6] By studying well, students serve their parents' desire—and God-given calling (Deuteronomy 6:4–9; Proverbs 1:8–9)—that their children become well-educated for the betterment of themselves, their family, and society. In studying diligently, students lovingly fulfill an obligation to honor their parents for the

---

5. Veith, *God at Work*, 49.

6. Korey D. Maas, "The Vocation of a Student," in *The Idea and Practice of a Christian University: A Lutheran Approach*, ed. Scott A. Ashmon (St. Louis: Concordia Publishing House, 2015), 103–12.

financial sacrifices their parents have made for their education.

Students also love their peers when they study. College is a not just a place but a community of colleagues, a *collegium*, where one student's questions and ideas challenge, shape, and sharpen others. Every student has a "duty to aid in the enlightenment of one's fellow students."[7] This is not a new idea about the vocation of a student. It was seen centuries ago in the Renaissance pedagogue Juan Luis Vives's rhetorical question about college: "What greater or closer union can we find than that of the mind of one man who is helped by another man's mind?"[8] It is seen today with concepts like Columbia University professor Andrew Delbanco's "lateral learning," where "students have something important to learn from one another."[9] Such enlightenment does not simply happen by bringing preexisting knowledge and perspectives to bear in collegial dialogue. It occurs by doing what the Reformation pedagogue Philip Melanchthon charged his students to do: "I tell you, it is your task to seek the truth."[10] To accomplish this, students must perform

---

7. Maas, "The Vocation of a Student," 107.

8. Quoted in Maas, "The Vocation of a Student," 107.

9. Andrew Delbanco, *College: What It Was, Is, and Should Be* (Princeton: Princeton University Press, 2012), 54.

10. Philip Melanchthon, "On Correcting the Studies of Youth," in *A Melanchthon Reader*, trans. Ralph Keen (New York: Peter Lang, 1988), 50.

two tasks: one, individually pursue knowledge, truth, wisdom, virtue, and goodness; and two, bring the trials and fruits of their labors to their fellow students in and out of class. In this way, studying serves your peers by edifying their minds, which not only helps them learn more and do better in college but helps them better understand how best to serve their neighbors.

The third *P* is professors. Students also serve and love their professors when they study. College is not principally about competition but "intellectual cooperation."[11] This holds not just for students working together—sharpening each other's minds instead of dulling them through sloth, cheating, and ignorance—but for students working with their professors. Students love their professors when they jointly share knowledge. Students should not think that they fulfill their vocation simply by attending class, listening to the lecture, reading the assigned text, handing the paper in on time, and the like. Rather, as the nineteenth-century pedagogue John Henry Cardinal Newman said, students should treat college as a "conversation between your lecturer and you."[12] Today, we see this in lively seminar discussions, invigorating tutorials, and engaging undergraduate research. Bringing your best questions, ideas, and research to class, the lab, the library,

---

11. Maas, "The Vocation of a Student," 107.

12. John Henry Cardinal Newman, *The Idea of a University* (Garden City, NY: Image, 1959), 440.

and office hours fulfills not only the obligation to
serve your fellow students but also the joint venture
to pursue what is true, good, and beautiful to love and
serve your neighbors—and nature—with your professors now.

Four More Ps

The three Ps of parents, peers, and professors do not
exhaust the people you can love and serve now by
studying. To this list we can add four more Ps: public, past, progeny, and your own person. By learning
deeply, students lovingly honor their obligation to the
general public, which, like parents, frequently funds
their education through state and federal grants. In
investigating the world, its questions and problems,
and researching ways to solve them for the benefit of
the public, students love society by taking its issues seriously and serve society by seeking to redress its needs
now. Even as a student you can be a public servant.
You can, as Benjamin Franklin said about education,
use your mind "to serve Mankind."[13] What questions,
problems, and issues could you be investigating now
with your peers and professors that can serve the well-
being of those around you?

Another *P* you can love as a student is the past.
Much education is spent learning the wisdom, folly,

---

13. Delbanco, *College*, 65.

ideals, issues, questions, concepts, experiments, discoveries, failures, quandaries, and resolutions of past people. We investigate the past because it helps us better understand our present and where we might go in the future. Students can love their intellectual ancestors by listening carefully to them so as to understand them fully instead of dismissing, neglecting, misinterpreting, and misusing them. To love them, students need to read virtuously. As English professor Alan Jacobs says, students need to apply the Golden Rule of loving your neighbor as yourself (Matthew 22:37–40) to texts in this way: the "book we are reading is, for the duration of the reading experience, our *neighbor.*"[14] In other words, in the paraphrase of literary critic Wayne Booth, "Read as you would have others read you; listen as you would have others listen to you."[15] Such charity moves students to pay careful attention to people in the past, offer fair and honest appraisals of them, and give due credit to their ideas and achievements. By studying this way, students not only love and serve the past but give themselves practice in how to listen charitably to their current neighbors.

14. Alan Jacobs, "How to Read a Book," in *Liberal Arts for the Christian Life*, eds. Jeffry C. Davis and Philip G. Ryken (Wheaton, IL: Crossway, 2012), 129.

15. Quoted in Mark R. Schwehn, *Exiles from Eden: Religion and the Academic Vocation in America* (Oxford: Oxford University Press, 1993), 63.

Progeny—something that comes from something else—are also loved by students in the act of studying. This can be understood in the simple manner that deeply engaging in your education now will put you in a better position to gain a good profession, which will adequately provide for your children. But progeny can also be extended metaphorically to communal descendants, all those later influenced and affected by you. You undoubtedly do not know how your studies and research will impact others in the future, but be assured that they will. All of us work in the dark, so to speak, when it comes to our future influence. One thing that is clear, though, is that the more we study now, the more knowledge we gain, and the more we learn how to do, the more we fulfill our vocation of student and the more God can use our learning to benefit others later. The history of science, for instance, is full of examples where the basic research scientists do in the lab is later found to have profoundly beneficial applications in life.

Finally, you love your own person when you dive deeply into your studies. While vocations are directed toward loving and serving others, we should not miss how God's Golden Rule presumes that we do—and ought to—love ourselves too. Loving and serving the self only becomes a problem when it turns into selfishness, placing the self above God and neighbor, serving oneself at their expense. But implicit in the Golden Rule is the idea that we do love ourselves and that it pleases God. Indeed, God cares very much for you, which is why God created you and sent His Son, Jesus Christ, to save you from humanity's fall into sin, sickness, and death, and deliver you to an eternally good life with Him in the new heavens and earth, just like in the beginning (Genesis 1–2; 1 Corinthians 15:11–4, 20–26, 50–56; Revelation 21:1–5).

So how do you love yourself by learning? Many students find much personal joy in intellectual adventure and discovery; they love learning itself and how it affects the quality of their lives. Take, for instance, one alumnus of Columbia College's core curriculum. When discussing the value and impact of Columbia's core at an alumni gathering, several attendees noted how this liberal arts curriculum educated them for citizenship. One alumnus, though, hastened to add that his education "taught [him] how to enjoy life."[16] Such sentiments are not novel; they are deeply rooted in the tradition of a liberal arts university education. The ancient Greek philosopher Aristotle, for instance, often commented on how personal happiness is encountered in rationally contemplating reality. We see the pleasure of studying expressed earlier in Scripture too, with the personal joy and benefit of studying the wisdom of God in His word and world (1 Kings 3:3–13, 4:29–34; Psalm 1:1–3).

---

16. Delbanco, *College*, 32.

Educating the Whole Student

What we have examined so far is that college students are first and foremost called to study; this is directly implied in the title "student." Yet, college students arrive on the doorstep of the university already having grabbed hold of multiple vocations. They have families with whom they are very involved.[17] They have jobs that provide them the ability to pay for some of their daily needs. They have friends who mean more to them than many in older generations can imagine.[18] Many of these students participate in sports and athletic endeavors, and are highly loyal to those social organizations.[19] In other words, even as students arrive at college, they are loaded down with multiple responsibilities that will, inevitably, influence their academic pursuits.

---

17. Jeffrey Jensen Arnett and Joseph Schwab, "The Clark University Poll of Parents and Emerging Adults: Parents and Their Grown Kids: Harmony, Support, and (Occasional) Conflict" (Worcester, MA: Clark University, 2013), accessed August 15, 2015, http://www.clarku.edu/clark-poll-emerging-adults/pdfs/clark-university-poll-parents-emerging-adults.pdf.

18. "Millennials in Adulthood: Detached from Institutions, Networked with Friends," *Pew Research Center*, accessed August 15, 2015, http://www.pewsocialtrends.org/2014/03/07/millennials-in-adulthood/.

19. See Hannah Schell, "Commitment and Community: The Virtue of Loyalty and Vocational Discernment," in *At This Time and in This Place: Vocation and Higher Education*, ed. David S. Cunningham (Oxford: Oxford University Press, 2015), 235–58.

Often times, these pursuits will come into conflict. Athletic practice might get in the way of studying for an exam. Long hours spent at work might mean that there is less time to spend with one's family, boyfriend, or girlfriend. This conflict often causes a good deal of stress, and even anxiety, within the student. Students today have been pushed to be "high achievers," and when individual success is not achieved in every aspect of life, students often feel high levels of anxiety, and even depression.[20]

When college professors and administrators insist that being a student is a college student's only, or even primary, vocation, many collegians resist, explaining that they have too much to do to consider learning their single or principal calling. Drawing on the biblical Lutheran teaching that all people have sacred callings in even the ordinary arenas of life, Wartburg College's professor Kathryn Kleinhans rightly warns colleges that "insisting that intellectual pursuits are more important than other areas of life can sound a bit like the insistence that the contemplative life of religious men and women is higher than the ordinary life of others." Kleinhans reminds colleges that they are educating whole persons and counsels them to be attentive to students' multiple commitments and social

20. "College Students' Mental Health Is a Growing Concern, Survey Finds," *American Psychological Association*, accessed August 15, 2015, http://www.apa.org/monitor/2013/06/college-students.aspx.

structures as well as the possible tensions that may arise from these varied involvements.[21]

Yet, if you are at college, then you are then primarily a student. And if it is the responsibility of colleges to educate the whole student, then it is the student's responsibility to participate in all aspects of that holistic education. So how is this done, and what does this mean for the student? The answer is a somewhat simple, though not simplistic, two-step approach. First, students need to identify their multiple vocations as well as the requirements those vocations place on them both qualitatively and quantitatively. Again, this is a matter of determining all that you have been called, and agreed, to do and delineating the emotional and time management costs associated with those endeavors. Second, you need to find balance while attempting to avoid what we will call lopsided vocationalism.

Identifying and Qualifying Your Multiple Vocations

Veith identifies that "vocation is played out not just in extraordinary acts—the great things we will do for the Lord, the great success we envision in our careers

---

21. Kathryn A. Kleinhans, "Places of Responsibility: Educating for Multiple Callings in Multiple Communities," in *At This Time and in This Place: Vocation and Higher Education*, ed. David S. Cunningham (Oxford: Oxford University Press, 2015), 101–2.

someday—but in the realm of the ordinary," which includes "washing the dishes, buying groceries, going to work, driving the kids somewhere, hanging out with our friends" and so forth.[22] The life of the student is similarly busy and full of activity both in and out of the classroom. Each of the activities and responsibilities that a student has is a piece of their vocational life. With so much going on it can be difficult or confusing for students to identify what their different vocations are and what kind of commitments each entails.

Vocation is a calling to any number of different occupations, relationships, or commitments. Since the field is so broad, it can be helpful for students to take a moment to identify some of their regular responsibilities. Doing homework, taking out the trash, and calling one's parents are some simple examples of the everyday responsibilities of a student. Each of these tasks is not in itself a vocation but is a part of one. Doing homework is a part of the calling of a student; taking out the trash is part of being a virtuous roommate; and calling one's parents is a part of the vocation of a child.

In order to see just how big a role your various vocations play in your life, try this short mental exercise. Imagine that you are making a list of all the things you needed to do in a week as compared to how many hours are available to accomplish those tasks. On the left side, list all of the different vocations you have,

---

22. Veith, God at Work, 59.

like student, athlete, friend, and musician. On the right side, note how many hours a week each different vocation takes. How many hours in the week need to be dedicated to accomplishing all of your "prescribed tasks"? Keep in mind, if you sleep an average of 8 hours a day, then that leaves 112 hours a week to complete all of your various vocational responsibilities. Most students will find that they are seriously out of time.[23] The question, then, becomes not only what are your vocations now but how do you responsibly balance them all??

Avoiding Lopsided Vocationalism

Identifying current responsibilities and linking them to individual callings is a good way to get a big picture of the vocations you currently have. But one of the biggest questions for university students is, What will my vocations be after graduation? In other words, Did I pick the right major? Will I get a good job? Will I marry my boyfriend or girlfriend, or will I move back in with mom and dad? These are serious questions

---

23. A student is commonly expected to study—read, ponder, take notes, memorize, research, write, edit, review, converse, create, practice, and so on—for two hours outside of class for every hour in class. If you are taking 15 units per semester, then that means you will be in class for fifteen hours each week with another thirty hours devoted to studying for those classes. How many hours per week have you allotted for your vocation of studying? How many hours do you spend each week socializing, working, or engaging in extracurricular activities?

with which students often wrestle. There is no simple answer to these questions, and, in fact, most of these parts of life are out of your hands. The future is not certain, and that's okay because each person has God-given talents and gifts that allow a person to work and find fulfillment throughout his or her changing vocations. Trying to find balance when approaching one's God-given vocations, then, is a better goal than trying to predict the future.

Imagine your life as a bicycle wheel. A bicycle wheel is actually a very complicated piece of machinery. It is made up of several parts: first, there is a hub; second, there are spokes connected to that hub; third, there is a rim that is connected to the spokes and in turn is connected to the hub; and lastly, there is a tire (usually a tube inside the tire as well), which is the part that actually makes contact with the ground.

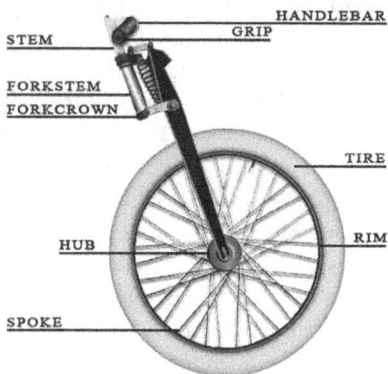

Each portion of a wheel is important in assisting the wheel in accomplishing its primary task—providing a mechanism for the bicycle to move forward. But the hub is the one piece that holds the entire apparatus together. If the tire is flat, the wheel still rolls, though it will take more effort to get, and keep, the bike moving. If the rim is bent, the wheel can still function, though the ride will be a wobbly one. If a spoke is out of true, the wheel will shake as it rolls, but it will still roll. But if the hub is broken, bent, or even missing, the wheel will not function at all. It is the hub, the center, that holds everything else in place and makes it possible for the other parts to do their job in turn.

Similarly, though students have multiple vocations, if they are a student, then being a student is their hub. It is the central calling that holds the others in place. The world of a student revolves around studying, learning broadly and deeply. If one of a student's other callings, say a part-time job, is out of place by taking up too much time, then the student's world may become a bit shaky. It might seem that the hub—being a student—is what is broken. But, in fact, what might be happening is a lopsided vocationalism that puts too much emphasis on an ancillary vocation, which causes the whole student's life to be out of whack. Jobs, family, friends, sports, student leadership, roommates, social time, and the like are all important and need to be dealt with through a student's multiple vocations. But they need to be attended to in balance and with an eye toward what it means to be a college student. To achieve balance in this time in life, though, means focusing primarily on learning.

Achieving Your Calling through Leisurely Activity

If you are a college student, this is the time you have been given to focus on learning. You have been called here to study. You have been given an invaluable gift to help you fulfill that calling too: leisure.

Leisure is often misunderstood in our modern world. Today we think of leisure as our "time off" to do nothing, just veg out or play video games. But the origin of the word tells another tale. The twentieth-century philosopher Josef Pieper explains that

> leisure in Greek is *skole*, and in Latin *scola*, the English "school." The word [leisure] used to des-ignate the place where we educate and teach is derived from a word which means "leisure". "School" does not, properly speaking, mean school, but leisure.[24]

What Pieper is driving at is that learning and lei-sure are intimately connected, not just on the level of etymology, but in reality. To study, read carefully, ask

---

24. Josef Pieper, *Leisure: The Basis of Culture* (San Francisco: Ignatius Press, 2009), 20.

questions, engage in dialogue, dig deeply, follow an idea, test a hypothesis, discover, create art, hone an argument, craft a paper, master a musical piece, and so on all require leisure in sustained amounts over extended periods of time.

We can put this into another context to clarify the point. No athlete would think to train just for one day before a competition. Musicians would see it as nonsense to practice once just for a few hours before a performance. Both understand that to fulfill their vocations excellently they must put in a sustained effort for a prolonged amount of time. To do that, they must have leisure, or free time, from other vocations and use it daily.

The same holds for the vocation of student. To perform your calling to study and do it excellently for the benefit of your neighbor, you need to engage in much leisurely activity. You need to find and guard free time every day and week throughout each semester. You need use your free time regularly to dive into all the learning opportunities you have in college. Better than that, you *get* to do this because you have the God-given calling and leisure to be a student.

Questions and Exercises for Discussion:

1. Get a piece of paper and draw a line down the middle. On the left side, write down all of the different vocations you have, like student, athlete, friend, and musician. Then, in the right column, write down how many hours a week each different vocation takes up. Do this for all the vocations on your list and then add them up. Remember, there are only 112 waking hours in a week. Do you have more hours in the week dedicated to what you *need* to accomplish than you are awake? What adjustments in time commitments do you need to make to balance your multiple vocations and live out your student vocation?

2. On the other side of the paper, draw two horizontal lines to divide the sheet into three sections. In the top third, list some pressing questions, problems, or issues that you see in your communities today—in family, society, church, or work. In the middle section, describe what course of studies you could take to address one of those quandaries now. Which classes might you take, and which major might you choose? What research project could you develop to investigate this? Which professors, peers, or staff would you work with in addressing this issue? When, where, and to whom could you present this? Finally, in the bottom third of the paper, explain how this course of study loves and serves your neighbor.